Thoughts Over

AF528720

Chai

WRITTEN BY ARCHANA RAJENDRAN

Title: Thoughts Over Chai
Author : Archana Rajendran

All rights reserved

All rights reserved by author. No part of this publication may be reproduced, stored in a retrieval system or transmitted in any form or by any means, electronic, mechanical, photocopying, recording or otherwise, without the prior permission of the author.
Although every precaution has been taken to verify the accuracy of the information contained herein, the author and publisher assume no responsibility for any errors or omissions. No liability is assumed for damages that may result from the use of information contained within. All legal actions are subject to jurisdictions of courts of New Delhi, India.

First Published by Hatchegg Publication in 2022
ISBN: 978-93-90446-21-6
Price in INR:
www.hatcheggpublication.com
publish@hatcheggpublication.com
+91 8766355652
Cover Design :
Aryan Verma
Distributed by:
Amazon, Flipkart, Manda Publishers etc.
Printing:
Thomson press

Table of Contents

The book Thoughts Over Chai is a compilation of some positive thoughts that is inspirational for everyday life. It is important that we are all surrounded by positive energy and thoughts on a daily basis. This book gives you a better perception towards life and helps you to a better living. They are thoughts about our daily lives and simple living so that we make a conscious effort towards being a better person.

Life Lessons

What does that bird chirping on your window or somewhere on a tree tell you.... There is more music to life than what you hear.

What does a boring movie tell you..... You either sit through or get up and go you make that choice

What does a good coffee tell you..... Go grab that hot cup of life and sip it before it is cold and stale.

What does the rain and thunder tell you.... When I cry I cry out loud only to make peace and happiness later.

What does the doormat at your door tell you..... Leave the dirt and get inside so you feel clean and fresh.

What does that old photograph tell you... There was a time you couldn't even walk.... And look now.

What do your old dresses tell you.... I may not fit you but I may be useful to someone... Like your life.

What does the night tell you.... I am dark not to scare you but to let you know there are stars in the sky.

What does your locked door tell you.... The key is in your hands... Just find and open me.

What does your handkerchief tell you.... I am fresh and clean to wipe out all the dirt and sorrow from you.

What does that unused shirt or bag or earring or cup tell you.... You are still left with one more unused chance.

What does a book tell you....I could be two things either your happiness or your lullaby.

What does that bottle of water tell you.... Every sip of life can quench a thirst.

What do strangers on the way tell you.... We are all here, on the same path... Don't worry.

Chance Taken

It's a vacuum of sorts
There is no pain
But no joy either...
No I do not want
Second chances at things..
And do not wait for
The unseen or the unheard
Neither the beginning
Nor the end seems questioning..
It's a hustle to start... And to end....
It's the in between that disturbs
There is a commotion... A chaos
In my passage of life...
Swirling in the memories of the past
And the want to that path of tomorrow
It's the in between.... All that chaos
I take a deep breath, I pause..
I take a look back..

I have the cheers of my loved ones

I smile... That's fine... That's fine...

I look ahead... It's empty.... Dark...

I walk along... I falter... I break away..

But the path finds me..

And I take a step.. A step ahead...

Towards my loved ones who await..

I step ahead... Into the light of my darkness..

I believe... I will discover the purpose...

Of my being...

Of my being…

Strength

I know no path
that feels like feather
I stood by the storm of pain
One beside the other
As strength
I know no time
When my heart was fearless
Of a fall or a slip
But I stood by the ocean
Of my own fears and strapped tight
I moved by the rhythm
And all seemed right
I lived...... That moment...
Everytime..... Just that moment

The Mirror

The fine lines you see
Is not one that has come off age
Every line is a story
Every curve is a piece of poetry
Every frown is a moment.....
Cherished, celebrated and fought.
The curls of my hair
Is the passage of my life
The strands of grey
Just a gone phase or
A wisdom that I flaunt....
I am not just a picture....
I am a mirror....
That you are looking into......

A reassurance

I reckon sitting by the window
Waiting for my children.....
Coming from behind and surprise me....
I reckon closing the door every time
Expecting smiling faces of my loved ones as
the doorbell rings.....
I reckon cooking a meal for myself
Something boring and insipid,
Expecting full tables during the festive
seasons.....
I reckon having nothing to do
But go back to old albums and be teary eyed,
Thinking when would they be back....
No I do not want to.....
I do not want to reckon the days where I sit in
present either thinking of the past or expecting

a future......

I will live every moment of my grey hair days..... It's a reassurance....

I will sit by the window to water the plant that grows there and smiles at me...

I would close the door to travel places and see happy faces.....

I would cook a meal and give it to some needy children and fill my heart with love.....

I would buy a new album and make new memories....

I would celebrate my grey hair days..... It's a reassurance.

Fallen leaves

Whisper the songs of people
Who stayed
Who stamped and walked past
Who sat and cried along
Who just held them in their palms and
Dusted them with a gentle blow
Who liked the noise they made
When crushed
Who just sat there and spoke
Spoke of their lives autumns and springs.
Spoke of stories love and love lost
Of betrayals and blessings.
Of tears that have dropped on them
And the crackle of laughter
That resonated in the wind that blew them
Fallen leaves have seen people hide

Their stories from people or

Shout loud about their miseries

Children who have played on them

Slept on them or crushed them

Adults who sat there and kissed

Who made promises of eternity

Of love hate and seasons to come.

Fallen leaves speak more stories.....

Paint my sky

I often wonder
If only I could paint my sky
My being with the colours I want
If only I could walk my stretch of path
Without having to hold hands
If only I could sit quiet without
Having to give an excuse
If only I could smile without having
To shoulder the burden of pain
If only I could talk without
Being misunderstood
If only I could dream of happiness
Without waking up to know
It was a dream
If only I could..... But I learn
I learn that......
I can paint my sky and walk
My stretch of path.....

I choose to be what I want to be
And not what you want me to be.
I am my being, my only soulmate
My forever then why do I care
Of losing than losing myself

Chai Moments

May not be that ideal weather
Of chai and pakode
Par chai ka Mausam kahaan hotha hai
Every morning you wake up truly
After that pehla chai
On a lazy evening
It's a Khushi wala chai
On a tired day
It's a chusthi wala chai
On a rainy day
It's a pehla nasha wala chai
Chai has no weather
A cup of chai can unfold
Million stories....
Woh nukad waali chai
Balcony pe bethke wali chai
Pakode ke sath wali chai
Shaam ki chai

Subeh ki chai

Woh wala gana aur aise wali chai

Biscuit ke saath wali chai

Whatever the reason

A cup of tea is just right for it all......

Cup or Coffee

Is it the cup or the coffee
Alright no debates
Be it the morning bliss
When the sun just starts
To kiss your forehead
Or a boring evening
Sitting by that French window
Your scribbled notes
And a weary song....
Or the night.....
A sleepless one....
No mundane thoughts
Or love roaring dreams
No goodnight messages
Or crumpled linen
Or a rainy day.......

That sparkles the grass

Or wets your stale bench....

Or.......

It's me who gets the first kiss

The love that pours out

Of her lips....

As she looks at me

Holding me between her palm and feeling the warmth within...

It's me...... Just me.....

After all don't they say

A Cup of coffee.

Love

It's a feeling that leaves one nurtured. Having said that, it becomes important to love thyself first. Unless you do not nurture yourself how do you nourish or nurture any other being. If you do not feel loved, how would you give love? A starving self cannot feed another mouth and a craving heart cannot heal or touch another. Look into yourself and love it completely, then you will be capable of only Love.

Respect

Something that only works on a barter system. You get respect only if you give it. The treatment you receive when you are loved and when you are respected is different. Every human, be it a child or an eighty year old deserves to be respected. However respect does not come as easily as love does. It's your deeds, your actions and the way you treat someone that gains you your share of respect. Respect does not come with age or stature, it comes with who you are as a person and how you see others.

Step before the leap

It is so important to take that first step I realised. It may be very-very small. People might mock you, make fun of you or even laugh at you saying.... Saying you could have done better. But trust me that first step that you take is your best shot. Because only when you take that first step do you take that leap. There is no leap at all before the first step. So if anyone is doing anything, anything at all for the first time, however small or petty that may be, appreciate it. If you cannot appreciate it at least stay out of it. Sometimes it could be your words that stop the first step and cripple all the dreams one is carrying in their heart.

Happiness

Happiness could be wrapped in chocolate, soaking in the rain, travelling someplace, being with your friends, listening to a song, reading a book, pruning a plant, sipping a cup of coffee or tea. Or happiness could be none of these but still being happy. Keep happiness limitless so that it does not come with something. Let happiness be your existence. Let your body, mind and soul be happy even without a reason. That is when you are happy.

A work in progress

I am a work in progress
It is slow... Very slow....
You may not be able to see it
But I know that every day
I am making progress...
It is my journey...
It is not a search in the belonging
It is not a progress unto the deepest
It is a progress of the self
Of my being.....
Of what I become
I am a work in progress.

My worth

Every day it takes a lot of me
To do what I want to do
Lot of the energy goes into
The others, the trivial, the belongings
Yet I gather myself
From the little that is left of me
To undo the rest and do the me
For only that gives me the ultimate bliss
The knowing of my worth is after all
The only soulful thing I present
Myself with

The choice

A lot of battle has gone into
The yes and no of things
What you choose essentially
Need not choose to be with you
But that is the winning game
To rightfully choose your
yes and no……
for that decides your battlefield
and your winning game
sometimes just doing puts
the yes and no in place.

Constant change

A little constant in the ever changing world
And we are bored,
We call it names…..
Bored, monotonous, usual…..
However even the constant is
Change into stability, into assurance
A preparation to step into
The forthcoming change…so
The constant could be
Just a recharge period.

Right balance

That's how you balance life
There are big days small days
Big dreams small dreams
A day sometimes on the edge
Sometimes over the top and yet
Sometimes sitting just right
Days that sometimes slip and fall
And sometimes stay put no matter what
Some days are a big goal yet
Some days the smallest achievement
Somedays that we fail to keep it right
And some that just stayed right
Stacking them all as memories
So that
If at all you fall
You can look back and see

It wasn't easy from where you build and stood tall.

THE 10 THINGS

How To Improve Your English

1. Read something small everyday... An article, a review, anecdote, fashion, food articles.... Whatever that interests you. Something small but every day.
2. Whatever you read write it down on a paper in just a paragraph. Don't copy the words.... Put it in your own words. Just a para.
3. Listen to something in English everyday.... News, songs, talks, interview or anything that interests you.
4. Pick up anything you have and speak 10 sentences about it in front of a mirror. Record what you say so that it can be corrected.

5. Whenever you can make your conversation in English. However small that may be.
6. Have someone with whom you can make a mistake and be corrected too.
7. Use simple words and sentences. A conversation is about convincing and not about how big your vocabulary is.
8. Practice English daily. Speaking reading and writing. Little but every day.
9. If you have to speak a sentence in English, it is important you think in English. Do not think in Malayalam and put that into English words.
10. Speak to your friend, to yourself, to your pet, to your teddy or to nature in English. Whatever you have in your mind say it in English.

THE 10 THINGS

Get rid of your complex

1. First and foremost come to terms with the fact that you have a complex.
2. Every time you feel less than someone in anything it is a complex.
3. If someone's success disturbs you it is a complex.
4. When these happen stop doing the first thing that you would.... Finding their mistakes and pointing them out.
5. Appreciate their good points. Try to accept what is it that they have done better.

6. Teach yourself that there are more successful people in the world.
7. Teach yourself that you are not bad. You are doing good, very good in your space.
8. Sit down quietly and write down 10 of your plus points.
9. Every time you attempt something or do something however small that may be make a note of it and appreciate yourself.
10. Always tell yourself you are not any lesser than anyone.... You are just not them.... You are you and you are different.

THE 10 THINGS

On the dining table

1. Lay the table properly.
2. Have everything on the table.... From water to waste disposing plates.
3. Do not sit with your mobile phones.
4. When serving yourself or others do not use your hand with which you are eating. You will dirty the spoon that way.
5. Keep tissue or napkin on the table.
6. Do not talk with food in your mouth.
7. Do not chew your food so loud that it disturbs others on the table.
8. Leave a clean plate as you finish instead of a dirty, undone or unfinished plate.

9. Enjoy your food and compliment the person who made it.
10. If you are washing your hands when others are eating do it without any noise. Respect the food on the table.

THE 10 THINGS

Self-care

1. Wake up early and everyday wish yourself a good morning.
2. Take a stroll in the morning. Let the morning bliss seep into you.
3. Drink at least 2 glasses of water
4. However busy your day enjoy your morning tea time. Sitting down quietly and enjoy the bliss.
5. Eat your breakfast in peace and then start your day.
6. Indulge in good talk. Be around good peoplc.
7. If something disturbs you say it and finish it before the day ends.

8. Do not crib about everything that you have to do. Either enjoy it and do it or don't do it today.
9. Before going to bed give yourself some me time. Listen to your favourite music or watch something or read something or talk to someone you love.
10. Sleep early and sleep in peace. Tomorrow is a fresh day. Don't carry forward today into tomorrow. Make peace with yourself before you go to bed.

THE 10 THINGS

Manage your household chores

1. Clean and spread your bed just as you wake up.
2. Use minimum vessel while cooking.
3. Clean the dishes as you cook so that you do not have a pile after cooking.
4. Once breakfast is done... Clean your home.... Sweep, dust, organise the things lying around, gather the laundry.
5. Everyone in the house should be taught to do their part of the job... Essentially and compulsorily.
6. Bring out what you are cooking for lunch. Cut, grind and keep everything ready before you start cooking.

7. After cooking clean the gas stove, clean the vessels, clean your work space and then leave the kitchen.
8. As you put washed clothes for drying and take the dry clothes... Fold them then itself. Fold them and put them in their places as soon as you take them off the cloth line.
9. Have your bath and relax with a cup of coffee or tea.
10. Before going to bed at night, clean the vessels from dinner and leave a sparkling fresh kitchen for morning.

THE 10 THINGS

Why wake up early.. 5 AM

1. It is the best time of the entire day.
2. You have the right time to take your lemon water or your morning glass of water.
3. You have time for a walk or some exercise.
4. You break your fast after dinner at an appropriate time and have your breakfast.
5. You have an entire day to yourself because you finish your chores fast.
6. You have enough and more time for self-care.

7. You drink less coffee or tea because you are more energetic and not lethargic.
8. You have enough time before you start your office work. This ensures a better prepared you
9. Be it any season it's the best time early morning to sit and enjoy your tea or coffee watching nature.
10. It helps you get a better control of your sleep habits and helps you be healthy.

THE 10 THINGS

How to manage your kitchen

1. Keep all your spices in proper containers and not store them in packets.
2. Always have an extra packet of things so that when over you do not have to run and buy.
3. Do not use the same pot for making tea and boiling eggs.
4. Keep separate pans for dosa, chapati and fish fry.
5. If working women then prep for the week and keep... Like making dosa batters, Chapati dough, making onion tomato gravy, cutting and storing a few vegetables, etc.

6. Do your prep work before actually you start cooking.... Like cutting, washing, grinding and keeping the masalas out.
7. Wash the used vessels as you cook and wipe clean your counter tops.
8. Do not leave the dishes in the sink for later wash.
9. Clean your sink, counter top and gas stove every day after cooking.
10. Deep clean your kitchen at least once in two months. A mix of soda bi carb and vinegar cleans every stain and grease well.

THE 10 THINGS

You do and not do with your child

1. Breast Feed every time the child cries
   No....Time the feeding

2. Run around the house to feed your Child. The child should know that eating is done on the dining table.

3. Putting your child to sleep in between the parents. Teach the child that they have their space to sleep.

4. Do not put your child to sleep at odd hours because they need to sleep early and well at night.

5. Do not use abusive words while in conversation in front of your child.

6. Do not force your child to perform every single thing they learn in front of family and friends.

7. Change their napkins as soon as dirty and wash immediately.

8. Take your child to the washroom at night so they learn early not to wet the bed.

9. Talk to your child. Grow with your Child. Read good things to your Child. Play with your child.

10. Teach them to put back their toys and books after playing or reading. And for all this finish your work while your child sleeps.

THE 10 THINGS

That would say you are confident

1. Going anywhere dress comfortably So you do not have to keep fidgeting With your dress.

2. Speak to anyone looking into their Eyes.

3. Before you start your point have a Glass of water and keep your calm.

4. Speak to the point and have all your Facts ready.

5. Removing your coat or jacket or
   Scarf or Stoll, do it before you start.

6. If you have a presentation keep it
   Minimal but with all the points and
   Be ready for any query.

7. Keep a watch on your mannerisms.

8. Practice before you perform it.

9. Any interruption in between... Politely
   Tell them that you would like to
   Finish your point and will then be
   Open to questions.

10. As you walk in look at everyone,
    Smile and greet pleasantly. After
    You finish look at everyone smile
    And thank before you sit down.

THE 10 THINGS

Why you should not have a child

1. Have a child because you are married for two years now.
2. Have a child because your parents wish to become grandparents.
3. Have a child because your friends have kids now.
4. Have a child because you love children.
5. Have a child because your neighbours and relatives are asking.
6. Have a child because you are at home and are bored.
7. Have a child because you will be 30 next year.

8. Have a child because you are financially capable.
9. Have a child because it happened by mistake.
10. Have a child because you need to prove your woman or manhood to anyone.

THE 10 THINGS

To teach your child without teaching

1. Stop using bad and abusive words.
2. Always pour water in a glass and drink.
3. Always take your plate and clean it after eating.
4. Always clean what you have spilt.
5. Always be ready 5 min before you actually have to leave and never be late anywhere.
6. Sleep early and wake up early. Read more. Exercise little but daily.
7. Put back anything you take after the use.
8. Talk, laugh and spend time with each other than be on the phone.

9. Do not bitch about people behind their back. Use sorry and thank you and be polite.
10. The child learns as it observes and not when it is taught through mere words and advices. What you do is what your child does.

THE 10 THINGS

It's Never Too Late

1. To educate yourself.
2. To pick up a hobby and learn.
3. To say that sorry you need to.
4. To let go off your ego and arrogance.
5. To learn to love yourself.
6. To start writing your diary.
7. To let loose of all the relationships You have tied around yourself.
8. To unlearn something you do not Need.
9. To let go of people and of emotional Bondings.
10. To live your life like how you want it.

THE 10 THINGS

To keep yourself motivated

1. Proper planning of your work. If you have too much to do and you don't have a plan.... You will never feel like making a start. A plan simplifies the action.
2. Know your most energetic time of the day and do most of it then.
3. Talking to yourself and telling yourself, it's ok..... Is a great motivation.
4. Do not over burden yourself with responsibilities.
5. Set small achievable goals to your path to the bigger goal.

6. If someone says something negative, smile back and tell them... It's ok... I will manage... It's my life.
7. Understand what you are capable of before pushing yourself too hard..... It's not about others but about you.
8. Be accountable to yourself for your actions and review it always.
9. Do everything to sooth your body and mind.
10. Tell yourself every day that you are doing just fine.

THE 10 THINGS

How to declutter

1. Clothes.... Repurpose your old clothes into something usable or give them away to the needy.
2. Vessels.... Do not keep old, broken, stained vessels. Give them away or give it to scrap or try a diy with them.
3. Old books...... When kids out grow kids' books, give them away to some school libraries.
4. Newspapers.... You can sell it off every month in kilos, wrap your good saree in them, wrap leafy veg in them and store, cover the books, use as gift wraps.

5. When you child moves to the upper class give away the books and notes to an orphanage to some needy child.
6. Organise your pantry every 2 months. You will find bottles and packets of unused things. So next time buy consciously.
7. Repurpose old bedsheets or clean them and give to the needy.
8. Do not store items for memory sake. Either use them or give them away.
9. Organise your fridge once a month. Keep only what you need and keep them in containers or wrapped in bags.
10. It's important to declutter your home at least once in a year or you would accumulate unnecessarily.

THE 10 THINGS

You do not do with a book

1. Do not hold with one hand while reading for that would spoil the centre of the book.
2. Do not flip the pages licking your fingers.
3. Do not fold the upper end of the page... Instead keep a book mark.
4. Do not leave the book upside down even if it is for a few minutes.
5. Do not underline the sentences or words... Instead write it down in a diary.

6. If you are arranging the books vertically in the shelf... Push back and give proper support or it will spoil the shape.
7. Once a while check on your stacked books in the shelf and keep it dust and termite free. Keep it scented.
8. Never keep a book you have borrowed... It is that persons treasure who bought it.
9. Never read lying down. Sit up and read.
10. Give away books that you do not use at all. It is better given to a needy than keep and spoil it.

THE 10 THINGS

You Should Not Do In A Kitchen

1. Keep similar looking spices in similar jars unlabelled.
2. Keep open packets of grocery.
3. Keep vessels into shelves before they dry.
4. Leaving cylinders on even after cooking is done.
5. Keeping mis managed drawers of spoons and knives.
6. Keeping food open.
7. Having too many plastic bottles or spoons.
8. Not disposing waste every day.
9. Keeping windows closed while cooking.

10. Keep a sink full of vessels and a dirty kitchen for the next morning.

THE 10 THINGS

To do before 30

1. Finish your education.
2. Get yourself independent financially.
3. Read at least a few good books even if you really aren't a fond reader.
4. Go on a solo trip.
5. Go to that one place you want to..... Never leave it for later.
6. Find yourself one good friend.
7. Whatever it is that you want to try a hand at do it.
8. Learn to love yourself.
9. Learn to enjoy your own company.... It will greatly help you in later years.

10. Age is no bar to do anything however.... Before 30 explore your possibilities and yourself.

THE 10 THINGS

To ignore what people say

1. Take up this course or that.... Ignore because it's your decision what you want to study.
2. Why don't you try in this or that college....... Do your research and find out where you want to study.
3. You have put on weight or lost weight... It's none of their business.
4. Walk, run, gym, yoga, this diet, that diet..... Do what suits your body, time and interest.
5. A girl should know cooking...... Well it's no rocket science and you will learn to survive.

6. A boy should not cry, a boy is the one to take care of the family, a girl needs to adjust, a girl shouldn't laugh too loud.... Human beings evolve in relationships and with time in life..... These are just societal pressures.
7. You cannot do this, you don't have to do this, you are not supposed to do this.
8. Get married.... And If you do... Then have a baby.
9. Learn from him/her, see how he/ she is.
10. What will people say, relatives say, they say..... Ignore.

THE 10 THINGS

To calm your mind

1. Take a stroll alone.
2. Listen to a soothing instrumental music... A flute if possible.
3. Light some scented candles or essential oils.
4. Write down what you feel always.
5. Sitting down with closed eyes chant Om. Or just sit quietly in a place.
6. While doing most of it you might have tears in your eyes if you are stressed and upset.... Cry it out.
7. Make yourself a hot cup of tea, coffee, milk, water anything that you like.

8. Have a good warm water bath. As you wet your head you will feel better.
9. Assure yourself that you have the power to heal, to soothe your mind, to ignore insult, to face challenges or failure and to bounce back in all your good spirits.
10. Sleep early so that your mind is relaxed.

THE 10 THINGS

When you leave home for holiday

1. Clean your home before you leave.
2. Throw away or give away any left-over food.
3. Store all open packets in the fridge.
4. Do not put off your fridge.
5. Take off your gas connection and seal the cylinder.
6. Do not leave bathrooms with water in buckets or mugs. Leave your bathrooms dry and keep the door open.
7. Keep all your windows closed but curtains drawn.

8. If going for more than a week do not leave vegetables in the fridge. Give them away.
9. Empty your trashcans, wash them and leave them dry.
10. Make sure to switch off all taps and switches before you leave.

Want to look Beautiful

Just wear a smile.

***

Even the skies cry

So understand

It's okay to cry.

You are feeling alone

It's just a feeling

Look Around

There are others with you.

***

Be the sunshine that helps someone

Bloom and Blossom.

Don not rush it… Growth

It's always one step at a time.

***

Be your own resource

Be your own lighthouse.

When your shoe lace unties
You tie it again and walk your path
Life is just like that….
Tie the loose ends and walk.

***

Opportunity does not come
Knocking
At the door….
Opportunity is the door….
Do not be shy
Do not be sceptical
Go ahead and knock it.

A string or a road has two

Ends

So once is never the end.

***

Moon is the fifth largest satellite

And yet is smaller than the smallest

Star… this truly defines Greatness.

Bookmarks are so that you
Do not read the same pages
Again.... But proceed further....
Incidents in life are our
Bookmarks to move on not go
Back to it.

***

On the road the mantra is
Watch what you stop on
In life the mantra is
Watch what you step into.

The mirror shows you your front

However

You need another mirror to see your

Back… it's a simple life lesson.

***

What is a Therapy

Art, Music, Dance, Cooking, Writing,

Yoga, Running, Playing, Gardening, and

So much more…choose and be your

Own therapist.

One needs a lot of energy
To cry and to laugh
What you choose to spend on
Makes you wiser and better.

***

Every decade of your life you are repeating
What you did the first 10 months…Lay on
Your back, flip to lay on your stomach, swim,
Crawl, sit, stand, walk, and finally run.

It's not just happy/sad,
Bored/busy or romantic/dull but happily sad,
Boringly busy and romantically dull too
So know better.

***

18. It's only you
Who walks the path all along to
The end
So love, nurture and respect
Yourself.

19. Like
Rains come down to
Nurture the earth
Tears come down to
Nurture the soul

Don’t strive to take the
Road not taken
Sometimes familiar roads
Lead to
Happier destinations.

***

Curtains on a window
Should only stop
Inappropriate viewing
And not the sunlight
That comes through.

You throw away torn
Clothes
You cannot wear what is
Not bought
So adorn yourself happily
With what you have…
Defines life… right

***

Tea defines love
Tea bags are restricted love
Tea leaves are open and
Strong love
Tea dust is residual love.

What you do should always be

What you want to do

But turns out

What we do

Is always what we are supposed to do.

***

Understand

Love is always on the

Other side of the road you are standing

And you always cross the road

In a hurry…

Only to be hit and hurt…

You didn't have a struggling childhood
Not your problem certainly
That you don't have a struggling
Adulthood
Well that certainly is your problem.

***

Your first stage is your own space.
Where you stand
And your first audience
Is the mirror
You fake it there
You fake for life.

You're a human

You are already 3/4th there

All you need is the 'E'

Empathy….

To become humane.

***

You are there because

You went seeking it.

Life doesn't throw anything

At you

That you don't seek.

You are the seeker
The turbulent waters
The scorching sunlight
The constant vagabond
The pleaser, the watcher
And the subtle human too.

***

If stones, threads and stars
Were to decide the future
Why would we have
Pens, swords and pasts.

When we step into someone's house
We are careful to remove our shoes
Or dust our feet
Take that moment to dust
All your ill feeling and negativity too..
Step in with clean feet and mind.

***

Growth is when we see, hear, and
Surround ourselves with good energy
Even the sunflower knows
That it can bloom only
Looking at the sun.

You are taught to shoot with.

You aim right and clear…

So is with words ….shoot them only

When clear and with clarity.

***

Every long journey

We have small halts to rest and

Prepare

Life is your largest journey

Take that halt once a while

To rest and prepare

We are like fire…

Get lit slowly

Once at its best… Embrace and engulfs

Everything

As it starts to die

It burns closer to its surface

Embracing nothing but

Ensuring warmth

As it burns out and ashes are left.

***

Someone's mistake

However small that maybe

Correct it, forget it, forgive it

But never celebrate it.

50% of our life we are
Acquiring
And the rest 50%
We are worried about
What we haven't
Or what even others have.

***

Any relationship
Gives you just one more person
But love is always within you
Don't go seeking it elsewhere.

We often have to explain

The reason for our anger

But not for our smile….

So smile for no reason at all

Just smile.

***

Only when you

Clean your specs the vision is clear

Clean the dirt the waters are clear

Clean the way the path is clear

And

Clean your mind the heart is clear.

The mountain doesn't shake
When you throw a stone at
It….
The waters do
You should know here to
Uphold as a mountain or
Shake as the waters.

***

There are many a slips between the
Cup and the lip they say….
The slip is when either cup (the point)
Is not held properly or you really do
Not know where your lip is (you do not
understand the point).

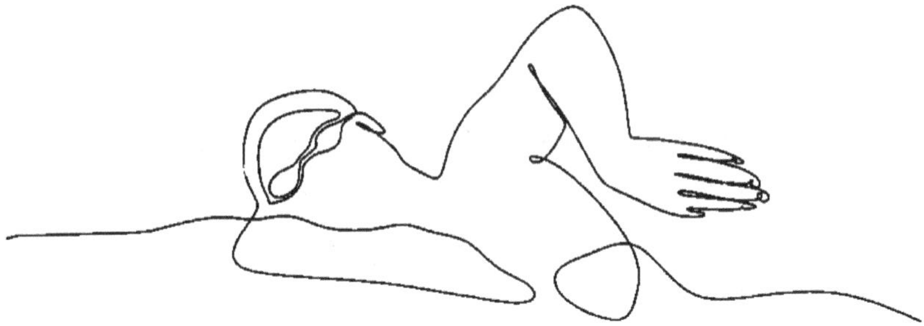

Turbulent waters are most difficult to
Swim.
It's best not to swim in those waters.
Just like decision making in a
Confused state…..
Best is not to make that decision.
And if you do..
You are taking a chance so be ready.

***

They say
Beauty lies in the eyes of the
Beholder
I believe….
Beauty lies in the souls of the
Beheld.

As a child we evolve so gracefully
And naturally, when understanding
Of anything is zero.
And when we know more we stop
Evolving.
We only revolve around notions and opinions.

***

It's human nature to crave
For sunshine in winters
And for chill nights in
Summer….
And each passes by with
Us only craving and never
Being satisfied.

To disagree to agree is human
Nature
Also to join the clan to agree
To disagree is
Human nature…

***

How to dance gracefully.
Well… step in when you have a point
Step up when you agree
Step aside when you disagree
And step out when you can’t take the steps…
Stepping out is easier than changing a whole dance.

You are wise isn't it…
You don't put your hand into burning fire
You don't throw yourself into a whirlpool
You don't see the thorn and yet step on it
You don't… Right? Right?

***

Only when you pull that latch
And open the window
Does fresh air come in… you detach
So remember to detach yourself as you
Age… from all locks and latches

It's more important to
Respect, understand and love
Human beings, than
Worship, fast and fight over
The unseen

***

Open up to broader visions of
Things humans, thoughts and spaces
Shut down to narrow lanes of
Things, humans, thoughts and spaces

Relationships are like clothes
That you wash, iron and wear again
Do not use them like diapers.

***

That first sip of coffee is life, That half a glass of getting
Cold coffee is also life…and
That last bit where you find
Unstirred sugar….Is also life.

If you need to put on the lights
During the day
You certainly are living in a cold
Dark place.

***

The black and grey clouds shine
On the outside as the sun comes up
And disappear finally…
Be that sun to your dark clouds and
See them disappear.

We have lead ourselves to buying the two
Elements…water and air
Let's not lead ourselves to buying
Humanity.

***

You cannot stand on your two feet
And entire day… Right??
How come you stand disrespect
And entire life time….

For any kind of virus that comes your way…

Pull up that mask and walk away.

Wash your hands off the virus and

Sanitize yourself with the goodness around.

Archana Rajendran, avid reader, thoughtful writer and a debutant-novelist, has had her career revolved around stories, poetry and English literature, ever since she was a kid. Born in 1969 and brought up in many parts of India, as her father was Officer with the Indian Air force, she has associated with people from different cultural backgrounds. She was a English teacher for almost 12 years of her life. Her curiosity towards learning and experimenting was never far from that of her students. Writing has always been a cathartic release for her at any given point of time. An enthusiastic home-chef with extra ordinary culinary skills, she also hosts the Talk with Archie, where she interviews determined professionals from diverse sectors, to bring out stories from a whole new inspirational perspective.